piano music repertoires

MASANOBU SHINODA

"Carbonic Acid"
for piano solo

篠田 昌伸

《炭酸》
ピアノのための

zen-on music

ピアノのための《炭酸》

この作品は 2011 年「中嶋 香リサイタル」の委嘱作品として書かれた。自分にとって 3 曲目となるピアノソロを書くにあたり、それまで探求した現代的なピアニズムを、「炭酸」という卑近なイメージにあて込むことで、より新しい地平を想像しようとしたものである。

I. Splash
高音から低音まで、休むことなく動き回るピアノを、いわゆる「炭酸水」のはじける表面の様子や内部の泡の様子等、様々な状態に見立てて書かれたカプリッチョである。

II. Ice
1 曲目と対照的に静的な 2 曲目は、二酸化炭素が固形化したドライアイスをイメージしている。前半は、完全に停止した時間のなかで和音が微細に変化してゆく。後半はそれが次第に融解していく様子である。揺らめくテンポのなかで、音は消失する。

III. Swim into Carbonic water
「炭酸の海を泳ぐ」と題された 3 曲目は、そこまで炭酸の様子を観察していたピアニストが、炭酸水の「中に入る」想定で書かれた。低音での規則的なストロークは、終始ペダルを伴いクラスターの波のような響きを現出させる。終盤に用意された繰り返しは、奏者や聴者が限界と感じるよりもさらに長く繰り返されることが望ましい。

2016 年 6 月
篠田昌伸

■初演データ
委嘱：中嶋 香
初演：2011 年 1 月 10 日　東京オペラシティリサイタルホール
　　　「中嶋 香リサイタル」
演奏時間：約 15 分

"Carbonic Acid" for piano solo

This piece was composed for the "Kaori Nakajima recital" in 2011. To create my third piece for a solo piano, my attempt was to fit the contemporary pianism I had been exploring into the image of "Carbonic Acid", something petty, in order to imagine a new horizon.

I. Splash
A capriccio piece with restless piano notes movie around from high to low, expressing the popping surface, bubbles, and many different conditions of "Carbonic water".

II. Ice
Contrasting the first piece, this quiet second piece depicts solid carbon dioxide, dry ice. The harmony subtly shifts in the perfectly stop motion time in the first half. Then in the second half, it gradually dissolves. Notes disappear in the swaying tempo.

III. Swim into Carbonic water
This third piece titled "Swim into Carbonic water", imagines the pianist who was observing the soda water, to "go into" the water. The steady bass sound strokes makes a resonance like clustered waves with constant pedaling. The repetition placed in towards the end is intended to be played much longer than the feeling of its limit both for the player or the audience.

June 2016
Masanobu Shinoda

■ World Premiere
Commissioned : Kaori Nakajima
Premiered : "Kaori Nakajima Recital" January 10th, 2011
at Tokyo Opera City, Recital Hall
Duration : 15minutes

(Translated by Lisa Sumiyoshi)

"Carbonic Acid"
for piano solo
ピアノのための《炭酸》

Composed by Masanobu Shinoda

contents

Ⅰ. Splash *4*

Ⅱ. Ice *20*

Ⅲ. Swim into Carbonic water *26*

"Carbonic Acid"
for piano solo
ピアノのための《炭酸》
I. Splash

篠田昌伸　作曲
Composed by Masanobu Shinoda

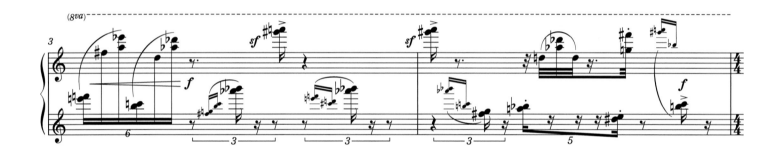
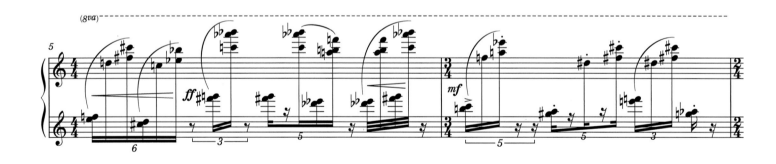

©2016 by ZEN-ON Music Co., Ltd.

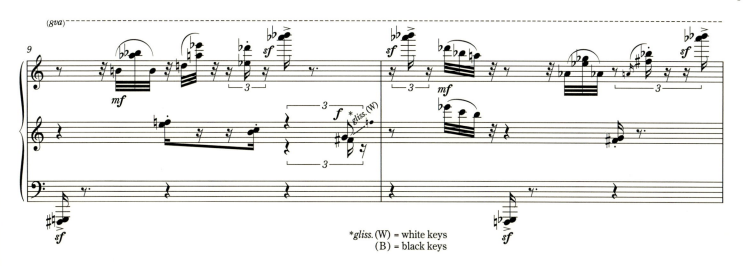

*gliss. (W) = white keys
　　　(B) = black keys

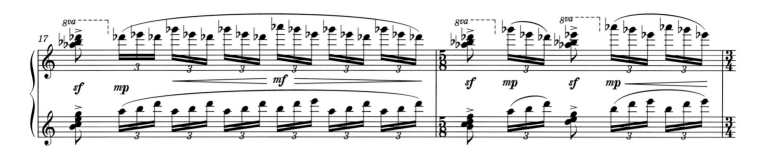
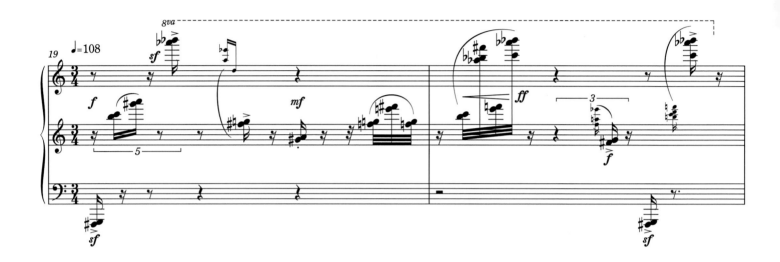

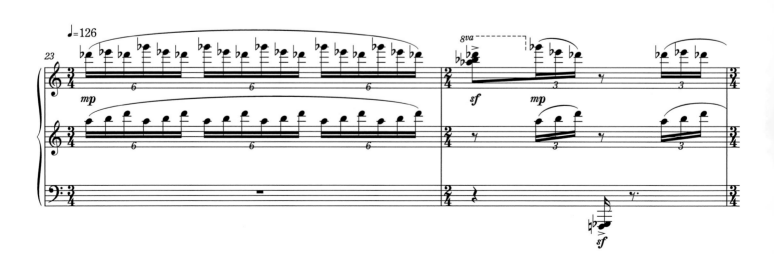

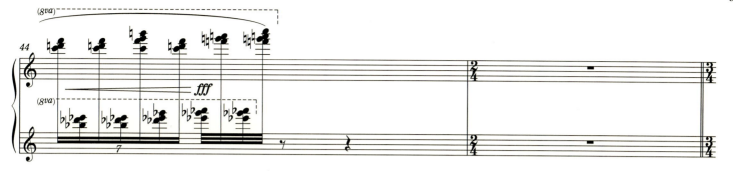

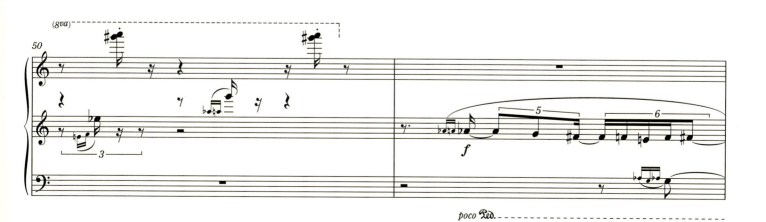

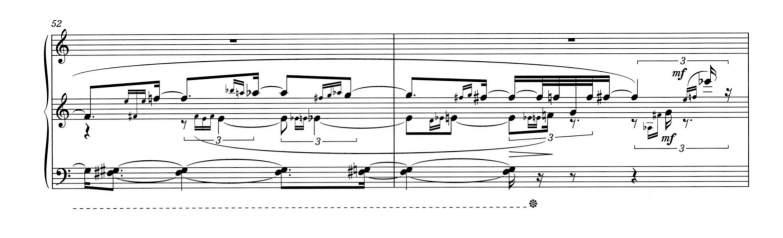

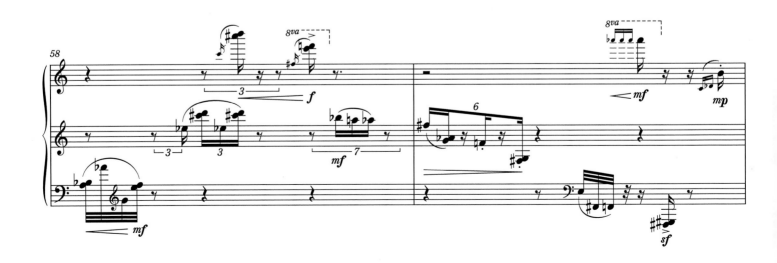

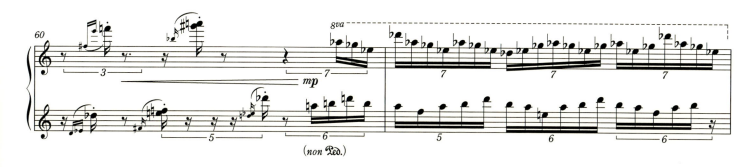

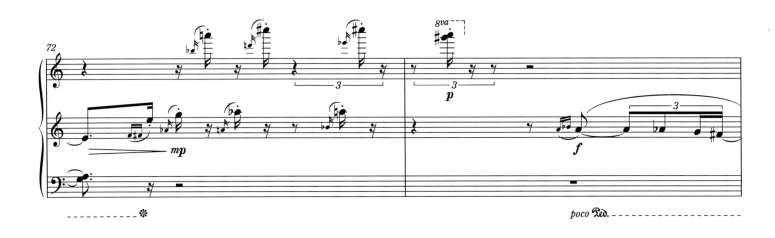
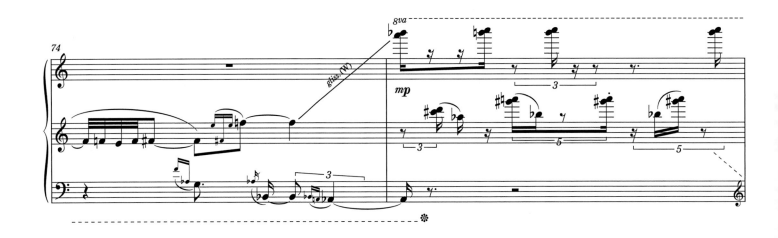

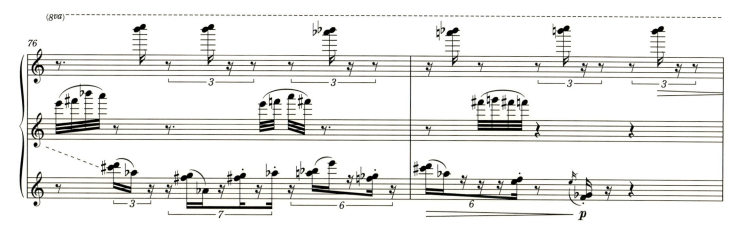

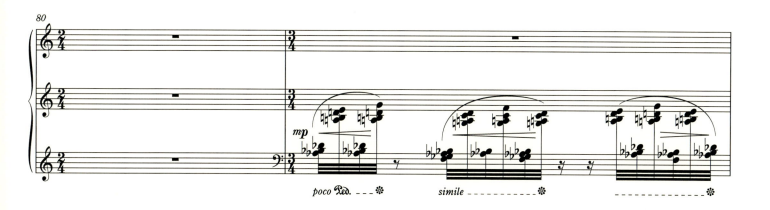
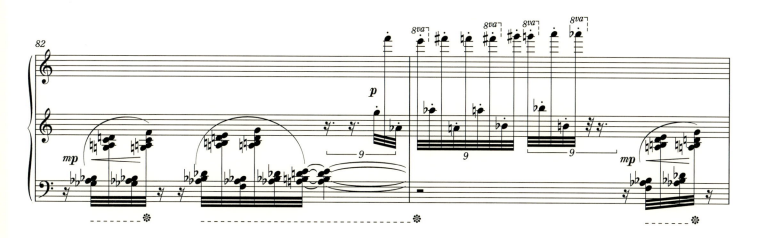

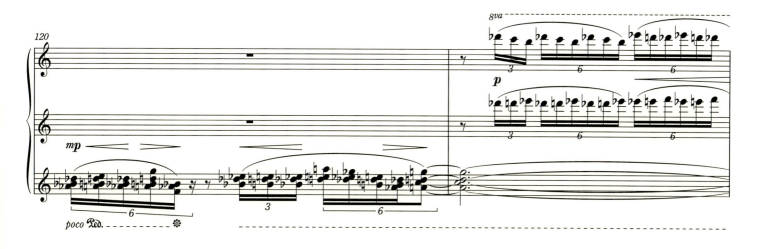
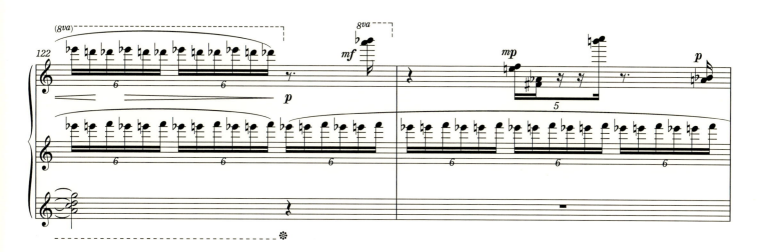
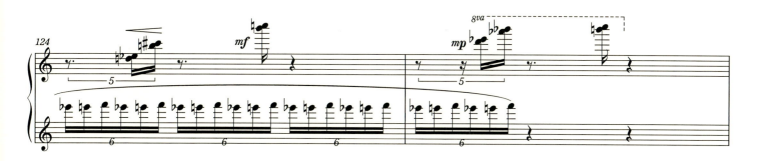

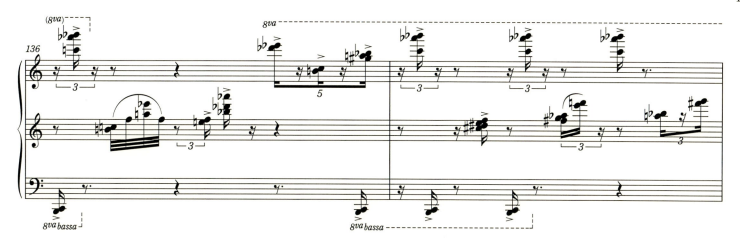

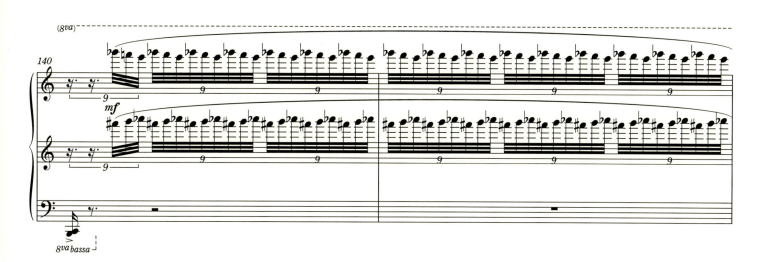
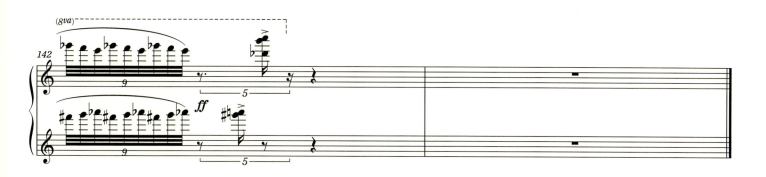

II. Ice

篠田昌伸　作曲
Composed by Masanobu Shinoda

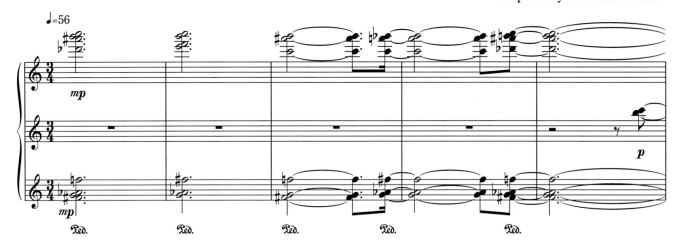
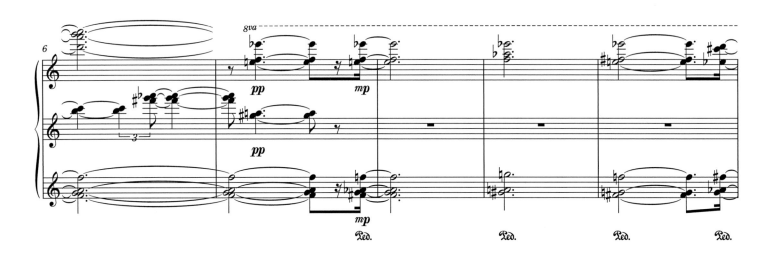
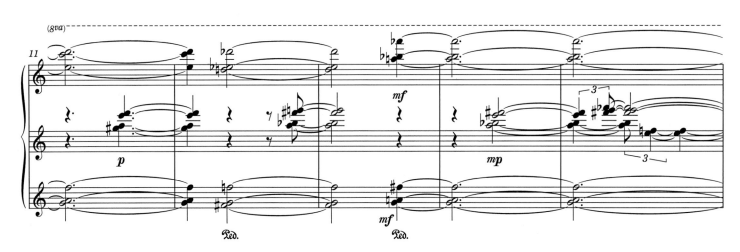

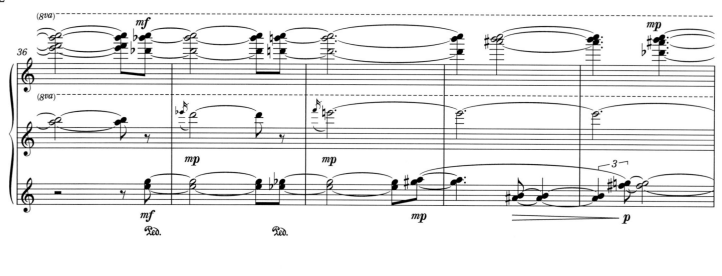
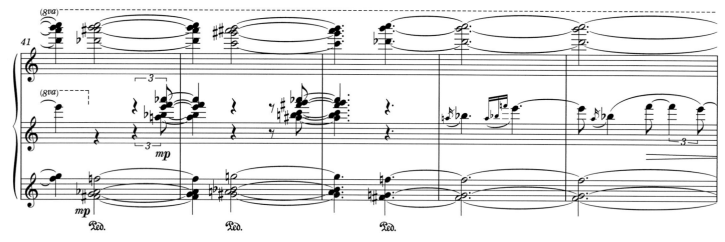
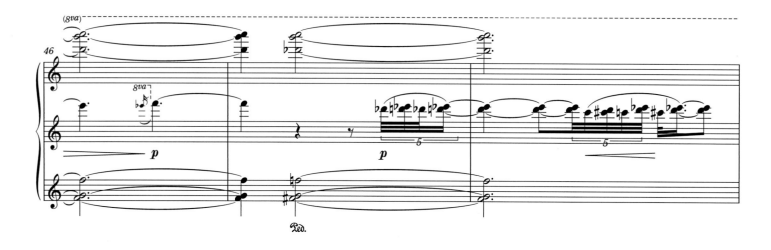
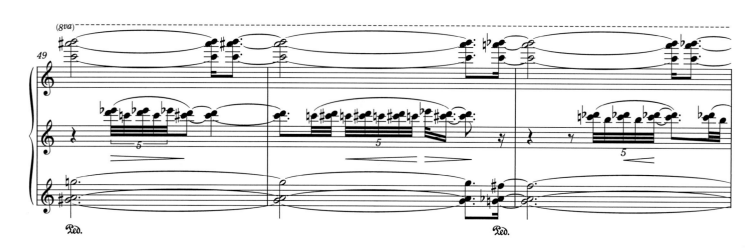

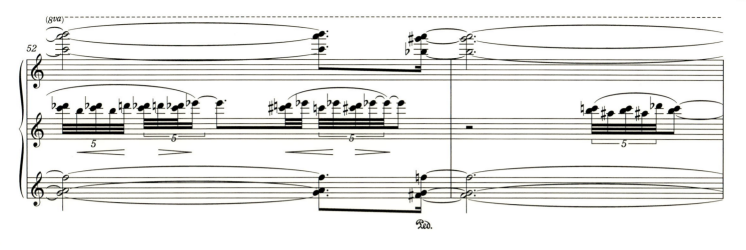

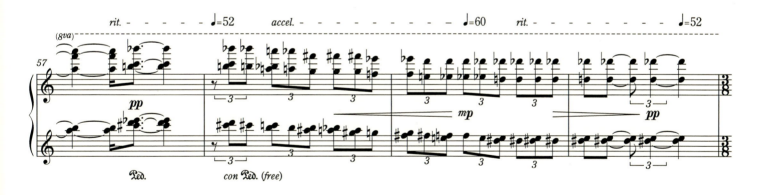

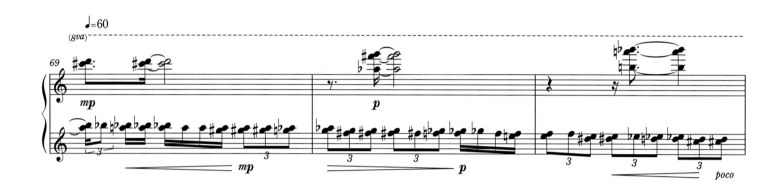
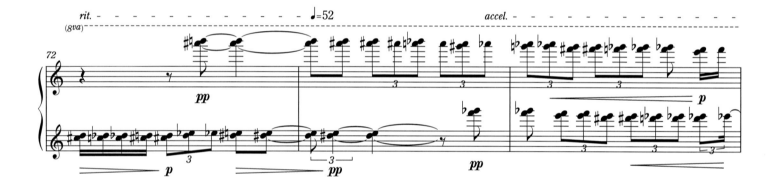
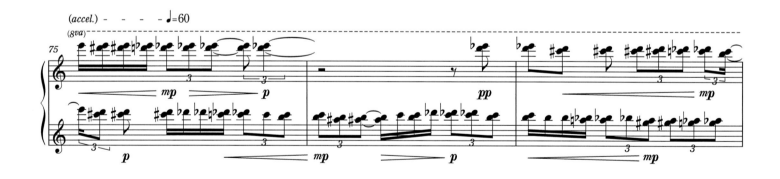
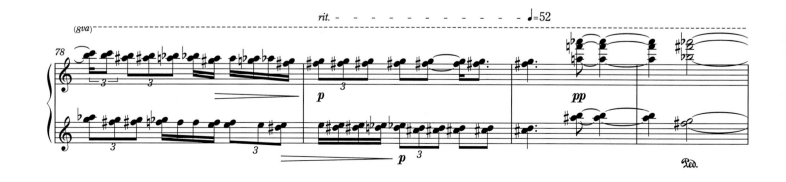

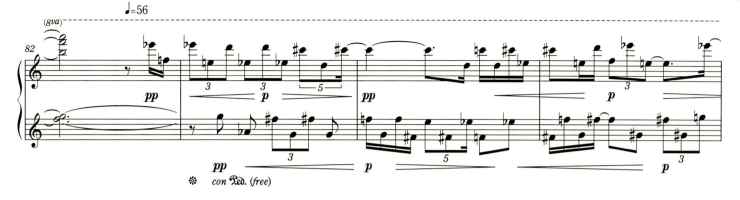
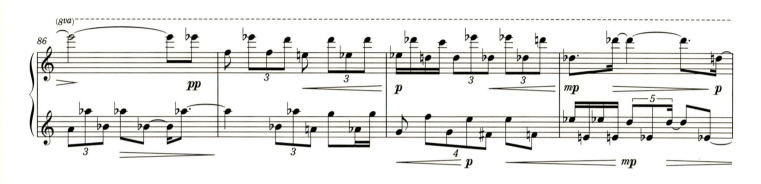
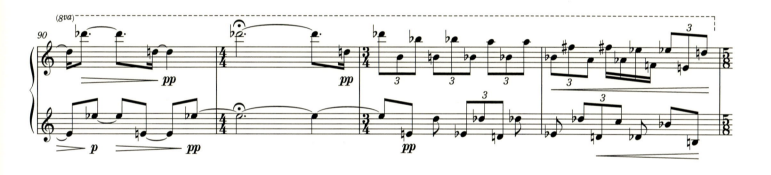
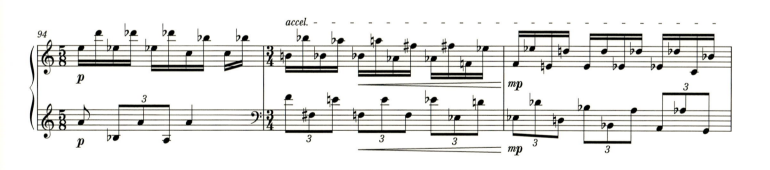

attacca

III. Swim into Carbonic water

篠田昌伸　作曲
Composed by Masanobu Shinoda

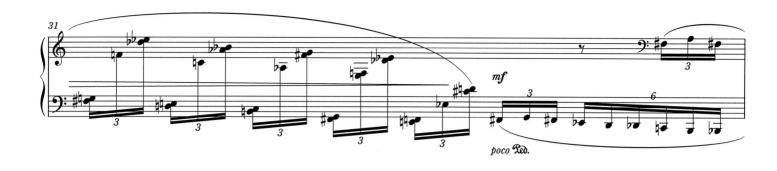
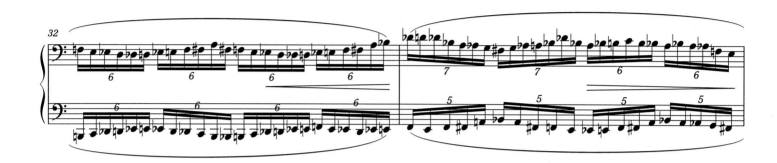
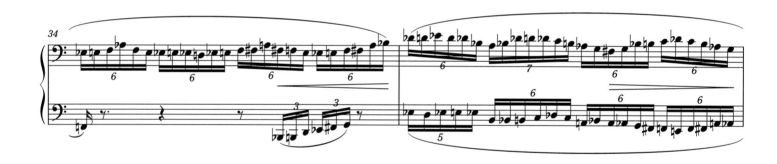

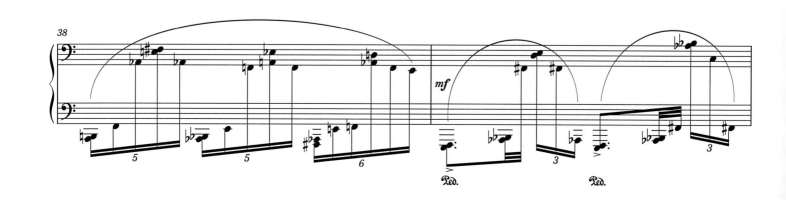

81小節から83小節は、ABCの各小節をランダムに組み合わせて繰り返し、10小節以上にすること。たとえばABCCBBABCC・・・等。
ただし必ずAで始まりCで終わる。最終小節のCでは、左手の最後のEFの音は弾かずに84小節に向かうこと。
また回数に関わらず、この部分全体でfからfffまで大きな cresc. をすること。

【作曲者略歴】

篠田昌伸（しのだ・まさのぶ）

1976年生まれ、1999年東京藝術大学音楽学部作曲科卒業、2001年同大学院修士課程修了。これまでに作曲を尾高惇忠、土田英介、ピアノを播本枝未子、大畠ひとみの各氏に師事。第22、27回日本交響楽振興財団奨励賞。第74回日本音楽コンクール作曲部門第1位。第18回奏楽堂日本歌曲コンクール作曲部門第2位。第1回イタリア文化会館日本国内作曲コンクール審査員特別賞、等を受賞。2010年、作曲グループ「Chronoi-Protoi」メンバーとして、第9回佐治敬三賞受賞。作曲グループ（NEXT、Cue、Chronoi-Protoi）での活動や、様々な演奏家、団体からの委嘱での作品発表、またピアニストとしての新作初演、声楽、器楽の伴奏等の活動がある。また、fontec、コジマ録音より、作品が収録されたCDが発売されている。 現在、東京音楽大学、国立音楽大学、日本大学芸術学部、尚美ミュージックカレッジ、各非常勤講師。
ホームページ http://ballad-filter.jimdo.com/

Masanobu Shinoda

Born in 1976, Shinoda graduated the Tokyo University of Arts in 1999, where he also completed his masters in 2001, studying composition with Atsutada Otaka and Eisuke Tsuchida, and piano with Emiko Harimoto and Hitomi Ohata. His achievements include the 22nd and 27th Encouragement Prizes from the Japan Symphony Foundation, 1st place in the Composition Division of the 74th Japan Music Competition, 2nd place for the 18th Sogakudo of the Former Music School Japanese music competition composition division, and the Menzione Speciale at the Concorso di Composizione Musicale IIC Tokyo. In 2010, he was awarded the 9th Keizo Saji prize as a member of the composition group "Chronoi-Protoi".

He works with various composition teams such as NEXT, Cue and Chronoi-Protoi, aside from other commissioned pieces for various players, groups, and also plays the piano for premiering contemporary pieces, as well as accompany for vocal and instrumental performances.

His works can be heard on CD recordings from fontec and Kojima Recordings, Inc. He is currently teaching as an adjunct professor at Tokyo University of the Arts, Kunitachi College of Music, Nihon University College of Art, and Shobi College of Music.

More information can be found on his website http://ballad-filter.jimdo.com/

(Translated by Lisa Sumiyoshi)

ピアノための 《炭酸》	
作曲	篠田昌伸
英訳	住吉梨紗
第1版第1刷発行	2016年 6月15日
発行	株式会社全音楽譜出版社
	東京都新宿区上落合2丁目13番3号 〒161-0034
	TEL・営業部 03・3227-6270
	出版部 03・3227-6280
	URL http://www.zen-on.co.jp/
	ISBN978-4-11-169021-3

複写・複製・転載等厳禁　Printed in Japan

1606072